Paradiso

GILLIAN ROSE

MENARD PRESS

1999

We are grateful to Professor Raphael Loewe and
to Jonathan and Connie Webber for permission to reprint
Professor Loewe's Hebrew poem
and the Webbers' English translation.
Acknowledgment to Czeslaw Milosz
for the five lines quoted from a poem.

Cover design: Charlotte Hodes

Worldwide distribution (except North America)
Central Books/Troika 99 Wallis Road
Hackney Wick, London E9 SLN
Telephone 0181 986 4854   Fax 0181 533 5821

Distribution in North America
Small Press Distribution Inc., 1341 Seventh Street
Berkeley, CA 94710, USA

ISBN 1 874320 25 X

THE MENARD PRESS
8 The Oaks, Woodside Avenue, London N12 8AR
Telephone and fax 0181 446 5571

Typeset by Antony Gray
Printed and bound in Great Britain by
the Alden Press, Oxford

Contents

Preface

Gillian Rose enjoyed the reputation of being a difficult author. Her first book, *The Melancholy Science* (1978), masqueraded as an *introduction* to the thought of T. W. Adorno, but readers looking to be introduced were quickly dismayed. The knotty prose and the involved analyses of style and reification were definitely not for beginners. Rose relished hearing stories from defeated readers of her first work, and would crown them with the information that it began life as a commission to write a *cookery* book. Her next book, *Hegel contra Sociology* (1981), combined a close study of the neo-Kantian origins of sociology and a reconstruction of the development of Hegel's thought in a synthesis that proved formidable even for those readers familiar with the arcana of Hegel scholarship. Her polemic against post-structuralist thought in *Dialectic of Nihilism* (1984) and her reflections on Kierkegaard in *The Broken Middle* (1992) in their different ways conformed to a level of philosophical difficulty that deterred many potential readers.

The recourse to a difficult style did not arise from an incapacity to write clearly – as testified by the limpid essays that make up *Judaism and Modernity* (1993) and the posthumous *Mourning Becomes the Law* (1996) – but reflected the working through of the intrinsic difficulty of a 'trauma within reason itself'. In the preface to the second edition of *Hegel contra*

7

Sociology, Rose traced the aetiology of the trauma of reason and her difficult negotiation of it to 'the dilemma of addressing modern ethics and politics without arrogating the authority under question', a dilemma which provoked the 'ineluctable difficulty' which she found played through in 'Hegel, Nietzsche and Kierkegaard's engagement with modernity'. The same negotiation of trauma is performed in the deceptively not-difficult *Love's Work* (1995), where the existential drama is explored lyrically through the experience of imminent death, couched in sentences whose rhythms esoterically allude to Shakespeare, Burton and Jonson. Rose relished the irony that it was *Love's Work* – her most difficult and esoteric act of indirect communication – that gave her popular success.

In the fragments of the unfinished *Paradiso*, published here for the first time, Rose continued to play through what she called the 'existential drama' provoked by the difficulties of modern ethics and politics. The work was conceived as a procession of twenty-one personae and themes, each provoking an affirmation of the difficulty of leading an ethical life under modern conditions. The few chapters that Rose was able to bring to a publishable state show a serenity and beauty that was always present in her work but rarely permitted their full voice. They are here published as her final word.

HOWARD CAYGILL

The flower
Sex, death and beauty
All in one

There is a film from 1937, directed by Irving Thalberg called *The Good Earth* and based on the novel by Pearl Buck. In this film Chinese peasants, normally eking out a living at subsistence level, are suddenly blessed with a bountiful harvest. Their response to their unexpected good fortune is to find it almost unbearable; they are terrified by its abundance. Without deliberate decision, the community pretends to itself that the crop is as bad this year as ever, in order mystically to to protect its precarious gift. This is a book about the good earth: it is my *Paradiso*.

I have decided that I too will be *difficult* for a few minutes.

It concerns your eloquent analysis of King Arthur's dream of Camelot with its tragic and inevitable outcome of sadness, no matter what choice he makes. The law that he has sworn to uphold will always rebound against his human weakness, whether or not he fulfils or ignores its requirements. However, as my wife Barbara and I read this, Barbara pointed out to me that there is a third scenario. What Arthur could have done is to pass sentence on Guinevere and Launcelot, but then offer to die in her place. In this way he would fulfil the just requirement of the law, liberate the two he loved and probably save the kingdom.

From a letter to me from
Dr Tom and Mrs Barbara Goodfellow
5 February 1995

Edna or the Song of Songs

MYSTICAL THEOLOGY

Rabbi Akiba said: 'Had the *Torah* not been given, the *Song of Songs* would have sufficed to guide the world.'

When I innocently and joyfully conveyed to Sister Edna that I was planning to write about her, the vehemence of her response took me utterly by surprise. She claimed that she would be ruined with her community, a closed community, which would feel that their trust in giving her permission to pursue her work on the *Song of Songs* had been betrayed. She wrote to me, 'What we are all committed to is a life of prayer in hiddenness. Against that I count my work on the *Song* as nothing'. And since then my love of her and my sense of the truth have been in deep travail.

My more or less immediate response was to point out to Edna that she represents to me the St Bernard of my *Paradiso*. In Dante's *Divine Comedy* St Bernard is to be found at a higher terrace in Paradise than St Thomas Aquinas; for, to Dante, St Bernard expresses the love of God, while St Thomas expresses the knowledge of God. St Bernard also wrote a commentary on the *Song of Songs* in the form of eighty-six sermons. The symbolic analogy with Edna seems precise; while her whole life-story closely parallels and modernises the dilemmas and the goodness of St Augustine. It was the desire to communicate her radiant goodness that gave birth to this whole work in which I am engaged.

Edna replied to my reference to St Bernard with alacrity: 'If I am your St Bernard that should make this easy. Bernard was *really* tough. Do you know the story of how, when he was preaching on one occasion, a blackbird flew into his face and, taking it by its wings, he tore it in two, commenting, "that is the last time you will fly in the face of God's word"?'

The violence of this threat to me opens up a surprisingly fruitful didactic.

In his *De Laudibus Virginis Matris* (On the Praise of the Virgin Mother, Migne *Patrologia*, vol. clxxxii, col. 56), St Bernard described the sacramental relation of the visible to the invisible world: 'full of supernal mysteries, abounding each in its special sweetness, if the eye that beholds be attentive'. This applies to the mystery of the blackbird as well, to the mystery of Edna's hiddenness, and to the mystery of St Bernard.

St Bernard was the most adamant and powerful man: he began preaching the Second Crusade in the Cathedral at Vezelay on Palm Sunday 1146; he silenced Abelard's anticipation of the rediscovery of Aristotelian logic; he opposed (unsuccessfully) Suger's plans for the first Gothic Cathedral, at St Denis, north of Paris, when Suger, who had accompanied the King, Louis VII, to Vezelay to hear St Bernard preach the Crusade, returned inspired more by the potentialities of Vezelay's architectural form for an urban and regal setting than by the call for the Crusade.

Bernard's combination of political power and spiritual humbleness, his combination even of the pride of preaching and the solitary devastation of prayer, are not mutually reproducing dialectical contraries that, in a superficially wise way, might be referred to a soul out of touch with its different strata. Let us leave it for the moment as the mystery of Bernard's visibility and his hiddenness.

How could St Bernard, the Mellifluous Doctor, be sure though, how can we know, whether it is not the blackbird who, with special sweetness, sings the Word of God?

I first met Sister Edna when waiting outside the Oxford Playhouse for a coach arranged for Jonathan Webber's first Frank Green lecture on 'The Future of Auschwitz', which was taking place late one afternoon in January 1992 at Yarnton Manor, the sixteenth-century manor house currently occupied by the Oxford Centre for Postgraduate Hebrew Studies. Edna cut a striking figure and presence. Acknowledged by many people as they arrived, she strode from person to person, lofty in height, wearing a habit that could have come straight out of a Counter-Reformation painting: thick woollen material in Vandyke brown, swirling to the ground, surmounted by a white coif covering the hair and ears, the bleached rope around the waist with the piece hanging towards the knees bearing the three widely spaced prominent knots symbolising the vows of poverty, chastity and obedience.

I sat next to Edna on the bus and told her I had just published a book on Kierkegaard (*The Broken Middle*). She had read Kierkegaard's aesthetic and religious authorship. From the beginning I liked Edna's combination of keen intellectual presence and unfathomable piety: she relishes expressing un-fashionable opinions as dogmatic truths, and, if challenged, will reason out her position without inhibition.

From the first we had Kierkegaard between us. Now, *Love's Work* is a profoundly Kierkegaardian work: it allows one to pass unnoticed. It deploys sensual, intellectual and literary eros, companions of pain, passion and plain curiosity, in order to pass beyond the preoccupation with endless loss to the silence of grace. Miss Marple is the code-name for this movement from loss to grace: Miss Marple is both exactly what she appears to be – a fiery, nosy, old lady – and something *transcendent*, someone who notices everything yet is not noticed herself. As a result she is not a 'person' in the psychological sense: she has no individual pathos, no desire to win the affection of others in order to assuage her own difficulty. She represents Nemesis – justice. Transcendentally, she is a 'person' in Polanyi's definition: 'To be a person is to be in the image of another Truth and to receive it and grow into it.' This Truth is the unpredictable outcome of the passion and pain of the characters in each murder mystery.

Miss Marple is what Kierkegaard calls a *knight of faith*, as distinct from what we mostly are most of the time – *knights of resignation*. The knight of resignation is recognisable: she cherishes her misfortunes, remaining loyal and dedicated to the mists of memories. She clearly lives companioned by ghosts: family, friends, loves and lovers. The knight of faith, by contrast, moves behind this all-too-human stoicism: she lets her lost ones go, whether injured or injurious, and turns her attention to the astonishing nature of what is normally expected until she becomes both invisible, hidden, and quite ordinarily visible.

As the sublime in the pedestrian, the knight of faith simply appears as whatever she is: she returns to her vocation beyond the endless anxiety of the test of salvation.

On the bus Edna told me in turn about her work in Rabbinics: how she had spent two years studying Hebrew and Talmud at the Leo Baeck Reform Seminary in London. I understood then that Edna and I had something else profoundly in common: a refusal to adopt or affirm the opposition between law and love which has so marred the development of Christian theology. By characterising Judaism as the Pharisaical religion of law and claiming a monopoly on the liturgical, pastoral and doctrinal notion of love, Christianity not only maligns Judaism but damages itself. For both ecclesiastically and dogmatically any religion will be operating implicitly with a notion of law. The result of the disavowal of this inevitability of law is that the Church, both the Early Church and the post-Reformation Protestant Church, become equally blind to the often inverse relation between the kerygmatic proclamation of love and the actualities of the law – to the ways in which the Church may itself be undermining its own institutes and institutions.

I understood from the outset that Edna's passion for the *Song of Songs* was inseparable from her insight into *Talmud Torah,* the learning of the law: that here was someone whose mystical theology was inseparable from attention to divine and human law, to the workings of the world.

A year later, in February 1993, I invited Edna to my inaugural lecture as Professor of Social and Political Thought at Warwick University: 'Athens and Jerusalem – A Tale of Three Cities'. She wanted to attend but permission was refused by her Mother Superior. The weekend after the inaugural I was briefly unwell, and then at the end of term I discovered that I might be seriously ill. Edna wrote to me expressing her concern but also suggesting in her bracing way that 'God is requiring you to go further.'

In Autumn 1994, Edna sent me an unpublished paper on the *Song of Songs* in which she concentrates on the soul (Hebrew: *nefesh*). She is familiar with the whole range of Hebrew commentary on the *Song of Songs* but her ambition extends beyond that: she wants to identify the intellectual and spiritual reasons why the modern world cannot hear this mystery of the soul, and hence commonly reduces the meaning of the *Song* to the measure of its own idea of the mechanical or the psychological or the appetitive soul. This reduction she attributes to Descartes, to Freud, to the secular and humanistic ethos of the modern world. I search for the way to say that this is an inadequate understanding of modern thought: that modernity is Protestant, not humanistic; it is founded on Luther's 'bondage of the will' not on Erasmus's 'freedom of the will', on heteronomy not on autonomy. Kant not Descartes, Kant in all his Pietism, is the source for both the modern world's destruction of the traditional metaphysical and spiritual nature of the soul (*die Seele*) and the reinsinuation of the 'soul' (*das Gemüt*) in all its divine precipitation and aspiration. After Kant, it is Hegel and Nietzsche who seek to reinvent the classical preoccupation with the soul, the city and the sacred for the modern world. In short, Edna's intellectual history is thin. I think I can bring her into the modern perspective by introducing her to Kant as the invention of the modern, critical spirit in philosophy, the philosophy of freedom, and as a Pietist, a reformer of the Reformation.

And I turn to Edna for help: I need help in my state of bliss. For I am well practised in the arts of resignation and in the prayer that they provoke. O God, take away this pain, this punishment – prayer in adversity. Yet I have no liturgy for thanksgiving, for praise, for consummation; for my well-being, love-ability, or for a new sensation; a constant awareness of existence, alone or in the company of others, imbued with a silly palpability, a beauty at once tactile and visual – as if on each intake of breath one were immersing one's hands in the deep folds of some fine material saturated with glorious colour. How to give this beauty back? I ask Edna if I can see her in order to try and speak to her about my condition of doxological terror. The withdrawal of the abyss, the overwhelming plenitude of every moment, leaves me more vulnerable than the busy tumult of distress: I have nothing to clutch, nothing to point to as my burden, nothing from which to beg alleviation. My soul is naked: it has lost its scaffolding of regret and remorse or even repentance: it is turned: and the unexpected result is the sensation and the envelope of invisible and visible beauty. This does not make me ecstatic, unreal, unworldly: it returns me to the vocation of the everyday – to Miss Marple's sense of quotidian justice – but it needed some response, some way of singing its mystery so that I can concentrate as ever on any fellowship or fickleness which presents itself.

Edna invites me to spend an afternoon at the convent: we have tea and cake in a small modern room at the front of the building. First, we discuss her work; and then she advises me to read the Halleluyah Psalms, starting from the end of the Psalter, reading backwards, preferably in the Latin Vulgate and then in Coverdale's English, the English of the Book of Common Prayer. Edna believes that the Latin is mystical, capturing in essence the spirit of the Hebrew. I find Latin easy, so I take the Vulgate to bed with me, and particularly enjoy Psalm 148, *Caelum et terra laudent Dominum*, where even the worms are exhorted to praise God.

> *Laudate Dominum de caelis*
> *Laudate eum in excelsis . . .*
> *Laudate Dominum de Terra . . .*
> *Bestia, et universa pecora,*
> *Serpentes, et volucres, pennatae;*
>
> O praise the Lord of heaven him in the height . . .
> Praise the Lord upon earth . . .
> Beasts and all cattle: worms and feathered fowls;
> Alleluia

Imperceptibly, the terror eases off as the repetitions of glory take up their abode in my hidden soul.

Two weeks later I spend a tremendous day with Howard in London: first at the Poussin exhibition at the Royal Academy, where over a hundred canvases are on display. Each painting, pagan or Christian, is dominated by its centrepiece of sacramental, cerulean blue – Marian blue, but the blue belongs equally to Aphrodite or Flora – promiscuous, unblushing blue. Then on to the Barbican for the Royal Shakespeare Company's production of *The Tempest*, with David Troughton playing Caliban. I fall for Caliban – like Frankenstein's monster, he is initially loveable, appealing not appalling, the excess flesh as fluent as Ariel's advertised grace. On the last train from Euston to Coventry, though, I feel I am surrounded by crazed creatures from Caliban's commonwealth, and stagger to the first-class compartment.

Relaxing my customary caution, I have eaten too much Chinese food, and am uncertain about whether I can keep it down. As I sit on the pink chequered seats surrounded by endless empty ones, the train straining against its reluctant rhythms, I begin to chant Edna's name as a prayer-word: over and over again –

> Think of Sister Edna.
> Think of Sister Edna.
> Think of Sister Edna.
> Think of Sister Edna.

The beat of the train takes up your name.

Gradually, as I sit bolt upright, the nausea abates, and this work comes to me. I will write a *Paradiso* which will be a series of descants on friends and family who have somehow passed beyond purgatory, who have dwelt in the abyss, in hell, and have undergone purgation. I will write about goodness and its fruits: under the names of Edna and Haríklia. And now the train lopes balmily homeward.

My model for Edna is the life of St Augustine: but not for the obvious reason that St Augustine led a dissolute life until he was converted; it is rather the continuities – the integrity and the brokenness – of the whole life which is relevant. St Augustine introduced the abyss, the dark night of the soul, into the Latin tradition, in the dispute with Pelagius over liberty and grace, in the Latin movement from the light of the Transfiguration to the solitude and abandonment of the night of Gethsemane. It is this Gnostic remnant in the life of St Augustine that has re-emerged, as it always does in the modern – including the post-modern – world.

In his *Confessions,* St Augustine sheds his Manichaeism – the form of Gnosticism he preached as a young man. At the same period he turns from human friendship to divine friendship, from the ethics of the city to the confessional intensity of the God relationship. He will return as Bishop of Hippo to exercise doctrinal and ecclesiastical power. The individualism expressed equally by his youthful wantonness, by the intimate *Confessions,* by St Augustine's effectiveness as the founder of the definitive theology of the Latin tradition, and by his institutional power, have left us ever open to the Gnostic temptation. To put it mystically, St Augustine's account of the third person of the Trinity in his great work *De Trinitate,* the Holy Ghost, the Spirit, who is the mediator of holiness – enabling us not only to perceive the change of the Transfiguration but also to communicate what we know – is *insipid* by comparison with his great evocations of the Father and the Son. To put it in literary terms, *the lack of irony* in St Augustine's *œuvre* indicates a troubled contrast between his appearance and his hiddenness, his power and his powerlessness.

Now, to invoke irony may seem anachronistic. Surely irony is the vehicle of modern romanticism or post-modern scepticism: a way of advancing a view without risking any commitment to it, a play of signifiers without any theory of being, knowledge or love? Irony has an older pedigree than this: I mean to refer to Socratic irony, to biblical irony and to their fusing in Kierkegaardian irony – that is, respectively, to philosophical irony, to narrative irony and to the irony of hiddenness and erotic self-revelation. St Augustine appears in his disappearance: this is the meaning of the *Confessions*. St Teresa's *Autobiography* somehow goes further: her mystical experiences, her charisms of levitation and tears, are juxtaposed with her institution-building, her organisational and managerial skills, her tremendous worldly power, in a way that enlarges our rational powers as it approaches the actuality of eternal life, keeping her soul hidden. As for Kierkegaard, he conceals his soul so well in the thirty-odd books of his authorship that it has not been caught to this day, when even the best Kierkegaard scholars attribute to 'Søren Kierkegaard' the carefully crafted views communicated by his aesthetic, philosophical, psychological and edifying pseudonyms: Johannes *de Silentio,* Constantine Constantinus, Johannes Climacus, anti-Climacus.

Gnosticism is our normal spiritual condition: pre-modern, modern, post-modern. It is the spiritual condition of those who do not consider that they have any spiritual condition. Originating in the second century AD, Gnosticism has flourished especially in the Renaissance, the Enlightenment, the early twentieth century and in current New Age movements. Enlightenment and the reaction against Enlightenment are deeply Gnostic. Gnosticism's humanism offers the alternative to the varieties of Protestantism; anti-Gnostic anti-humanism offers an exoteric, psychological soteriological humanism in the place of grace.

'And I believed (wretch that I was) that more mercy was to be shown to the fruits of the earth, than unto men for whose use they were created . . . Had some Manichean saint eaten, he should digest in his guts, and breath out of that fog, very angels: yea, in his prayer, groan and sigh out certain portions, forsooth, of the Deity: as if portions of the Most High and True God should remain bound in that fog unless they had been set at liberty by the teeth or belly of some elect holy one.'

The Manichean doctrine which St Augustine here ridicules is that of *Jesus patibilis,* the 'passible' or suffering Jesus who is dispersed in all creation: his most genuine realm and embodiment seems to be the vegetable world, that is, the most passive and the only innocent form of life. Actively, Jesus is transcendent *Nous* who, coming from above, liberates this captive substance and continually until the end of the world collects it, that is, himself, out of the physical dispersal.

Gnosticism in its many varieties holds that knowledge, *gnosis,* is the key to human salvation. This knowledge is not *amata notitia,* Augustine's 'loved knowledge'; for Gnosticism, knowledge liberates the self from its bonds in opposition to love of the neighbour, to the intensification of soul bonding. *Gnosis* is posited on the radical nature of Evil in opposition to the radical nature of the Good. If the Good is radical, then Evil is a privation of the good, *privatio boni,* an aversion, a turning away from the Good. Evil on this view has no independent reality. According to Gnosticism, Evil is *sui generis,* an independent principle belonging to material reality, to eternal, autonomous material substance. Gnosticism is founded on dualisms: of matter and reason, of body and soul. The individual requires illumination, wisdom, knowledge, *gnosis,* in order to set free the spark of the divine inhabiting each imprisoned being. Ignorance is the only fallen condition, not sin.

Gnosticism offers a catastrophic cosmogony: creation is not the work of a loving God, for the Godhead is infinitely removed. Primal man is deposited by maleficient demiurgic Aeons, epochs or ages, who dominate myriad realms of cosmic disorder in space.

Gnosticism is insidiously compelling, whether we harbour it unself-consciously as our commonsense, or whether we embrace it in one of its doctrinal forms. Many people in all ages hover between the commonsensical and the doctrinal. 'Know thyself', the ancient Greek motto, still provides the call for the exercise of reason to fathom the irrational, for the emphasis on the isolated self separate from community and corporation, for the dualisms, which modernity has reinvented, between the body and the soul, matter and spirit, nature and culture. These 'commonsensical' assumptions reassure us that we need only to overcome ignorance, we are not beset by sin; that knowledge will empower us, whereas love deprives us of power; that evil is ineluctable, intrinsic to the world as such, and not the consequence of our own misguided agency. Gnosticism exalts its mysticism of knowledge against the background of the disordered polis and the disordered cosmos: the disaster – *disaster* means the tearing out of the stars – is opposed to the harmonious music of the spheres. This disharmony is projected from global political disarray: the polis is lost, the Republic is betrayed, the world-order displays an anarchic infinity of internecine forces.

Gnosticism is as compelling today as it was in the second century AD.

In his youth, St Augustine was a confirmed Gnostic: he belonged to the most organised and widespread Gnostic church, the Church of the Manichees, followers of Mani, the Gnostic sage. After his conversion to Christianity, Augustine wrote tireless Latin polemics against the Gnostics as the Greek fathers had done before him. Augustine's controversy with the Christian Pelagius, reflected in Reformation debates between Erasmus and Luther, raises a Christian version of a comparable issue. Pelagius does not, of course, defend knowledge as the road to salvation, but he does defend the contribution of individual effort towards the merit of grace, whereas Augustine, like Luther, denies the efficacy of the individual will in achieving salvation. He denies the value of human autonomy altogether, regardless of the consequent quiescent ethical implications which so troubled Pelagius and Erasmus.

Augustine's hiddenness, preserved not betrayed by his *Confessions,* and his powerfulness as theologian and bishop, is mediated by his mother, Monica. Augustine, even in his most dissolute and abandoned moments, is held by her in the deepest recesses of his agonies, in the ethical life of early friendship, in the quasi-ethical life with his concubine and son, in his studies and conversion and in his accession to institutional power. Both before and after her death, he is held by Monica and he is holding Monica, who was herself a paradox of hiddenness and powerfulness − which is the full meaning of piety. This meditated and mediating mothering softens the trouble in the middle between Augustine's hiddenness and his visible power.

This trouble was discerned in his presentation of the Holy Spirit, the third person and mediator of the Trinity, who is breathing and virtue, communication and community, and in his trouble with irony generally − his difficulty as it were, with the irony of the Trinity itself. *Patres comederunt uvam acerbam, et dentes filiorum obstupescunt.* The fathers have eaten sour grapes, and the children's teeth are set on edge. (Ezekiel 18:2, cited in St Augustine's *Enchiridion on Faith, Hope and Love.*)

Augustine takes this arresting proverb of Israel to contrast its ethos with the Christian second birth which liberates individuals from the sins and guilt of the fathers, and from the first sin 'passed upon all men'. Yet Ezekiel is himself announcing God's abrogation of this proverb in Israel:

> *Ecce omnes animae meae sunt.*
> Behold. all souls are mine.
>
> Ezekiel, 18:4

Edna has gone further than St Augustine: she would never divest and confiscate Judaism of the treasures which Christianity has purloined. For Edna, mystical theologian, engages equally in *Talmud Torah,* the searching of the law. Her hiddenness and her public presence, her power, are held in this mediation, more truly triune than any unironic, truncated trinitarianism.

Edna was born in 1931 to impecunious Bohemian parents. Her father, a critic and novelist, was at a low ebb when he married the daughter of two music-hall artistes and a revue dancer in London and Paris. His wife, however, had educated herself, and by the time Edna, her second child and first daughter, was born, she had become deeply involved with psychoanalysis and was starting to practise as a lay analyst.

Edna inherited and made her own her mother's love of dance: she trained in classical ballet, dancing in Paris and on tour throughout Italy as well as in London. Until she was twenty-five years old, Edna was dedicated to the austere discipline of classical ballet. For the next ten years Edna combined dancing with fashion modelling. A few remaining photographs show her in Wili-like Giselle poses with demurely inclined head, then large and lofty in evening dress, in full and brazen confrontation with the camera.

From her mother Edna also took on an intense and exclusive spirituality, the alternative religion of the day: Gnosticism. While her mother, much later, co-authored with her third husband, a biography of the India guru, Meher Baba, the household of Edna's youth, as it moved from Geneva to London, followed the passionate discipline of Gurdjieff, as his teaching was classically presented in P. D. Ouspensky's *In Search of the Miraculous: Fragments of an Unknown Teaching.*

'Of the desires expressed the one which is most right is the desire to be *master of oneself,* because without this nothing else is possible . . . in order to help others one must first learn to be a conscious egoist. Only a conscious egoist can help people.'

Ouspensky's account of Gurdjieff's teaching is set in St Petersburg and London in the period of the First World War from 1915 to 1917. He presents himself as an initiate to Gurdjieff's system of knowledge. Formulated in opposition to the bodily ascetic and motionless way of the fakir, the emotionally obedient and servile way of the monk, and the cerebrally exclusive way of the yogi, Gurdjieff teaches self-mastery. This conception of self-mastery involves an overcoming of that mechanical life in which man's name is legion: a theosophical ascent through the four increasingly finer planes, of the physical, the astral, the mental, the divine, through the body, the desire, the mind, to the mastering consciousness or will – to immortality. This immortality is acquired only by means of terribly hard inner work and struggle.

Like earlier gnosticisms, Gurdjieff's system is individualistic ('egoistic', to cite its own term); it implies a dualism between the lost, mechanistic, material world and the Whole or One or All, whose single will employs the three forces, positive, negative and neutralising, to create a number of worlds.

Analogous to classic gnosticisms, much of the energy of Ouspensky's exposition of Gurdjieff's system is spent on an increasingly elaborate cosmology of worlds and ages.

This overwhelming preoccupation with labyrinthine cosmology may have contributed to Ouspensky's break with Gurdjieff after 1917. His book begins and ends on the same note: he first heard of Gurdjieff in a Moscow newspaper in 1914 announcing the latter's attempt in St Petersburg to stage a ballet, *The Struggle of the Magicians*, a presentation of Oriental miracle and Sufi sacred dance, set in India. He parts from Gurdjieff in 1922 as Gurdjieff is working again in Paris and London on the preparation of this ballet.

In London, Edna, as a young adult, dancer and model, continued her childhood upbringing in Gnosticism by attending classes with unfailing regularity at the School of Economic Science (SES) based on Ouspensky's work. She considered the system of knowledge with its promise of individual *gnosis* to be far superior to Christian values.

If purity of heart is to will one thing, then Edna did not take any inheritance from her extravagant mother. The ballerina and fashion model would seem to invite the admiring gaze of her audience; she would appear to crave public desire and recognition. Yet the young woman who inhabited, indeed dominated, such a visible, even promiscuous world was immaculate: immaculate in the distance cultivated daily in the rigours of the dance, immaculate in the defiance wrapped in satin, silk and furs. Gnosticism preserved this invisible soul, providing a system of self-mastery which dovetailed with the control and cultivation of the presentation of her body. All three systems, ballet, modelling and Gnosticism, continuously practised programmes, produce a proficient performer, who monitors herself day and night with both her visible and her invisible eye. Like the young St Augustine, the young Edna was initially empowered and hidden by these self-centred *gnoses* – *gnoses* which she would come to see as deficient in faith, hope and love. Unlike St Augustine, her mother could not show her the way forward. And Edna will not be able to sing the *Song of Songs* until she abandons this all too Greek *gnosis*, and allows herself to become less immaculate, to allow the imperfections throughout her physical and moral being to exist. Only then is she truly hidden and infinitely bounteous in her appearing.

Meanwhile the armour of Gnosticism furnished the mind as well as the body with its chivalric *hauteur* for a chaste mission in an unchaste world.

One day, a good friend of Edna's asked her if she would like to act as godparent to the child she (the friend) was expecting. Edna accepted the role without reflecting on its implications, although she was neither baptised nor confirmed. She approached a local pastor and asked, without more ado, to be baptised. Her insouciance did not go unchallenged: she was informed that a course of instruction was the essential preparation for reception into the Church of England.

Let us leave this soul hidden: Edna expresses what happened as a war breaking out between the Gnostic securities and the uncertainties of Christianity. For faith is first and last negative capability, as Keats puts it, the capacity of being in uncertainties, mysteries, doubts, without any irritable reaching after fact and reasons. It is also positive capability, not developed by Keats, the enlarging of inhibited reason in the domain of praxis, of practical reason, Aristotle's *phronesis,* the educating of wisdom that knows when to pass unnoticed and when to act.

At the age of thirty-five Edna joined an Anglican order founded in 1906 that follows the Benedictine Rule and uses the Catholic Missal. While it is a closed, contemplative order, a small number of the sisters are scholars, most frequently historians of the Church. Edna, however, is a mystical theologian, where mystery means revelation not esoteric knowledge or practice. Her main foci of interest are fourfold. First, the Greek fathers: Origen, Irenaeus, Gregory of Nyssa, Maximus the Confessor; second, the great Latins: St Augustine, above all, but also St Teresa of Avila and St John of the Cross; third, Rabbinic Judaism of the *Mishnah* and *Talmud*; and, finally, welding and overarching all these, the Hebrew *Song of Songs* and the Hebrew Scriptures. Edna is profoundly alert to anachronism: to the historical and spiritual projection of modern, sceptical Enlightenment and post-Enlightenment methods of biblical interpretation and of interpretation generally, whether on to the Hebrew Scripture or theology. Peter Brown's highly acclaimed life of St Augustine provoked her deepest crisis of faith. Brown, for all his impeccable scholarship, writes a reductive 'literary' biography, where every stage in the development of Augustine's life and thought is attributed to the change in his age – to his youth, to his maturity, to his ageing. This is a pitiful approach to *any* life, ancient or modern, prophet, preacher or poet, that has been productive of a body of work challenging our reductive ideas of what a life can be. The meaning of the work opens up the meaning of life. Psychic distress, with which we are so doggedly familiar, is enlisted in the ineluctable paradox displayed in every life of power and powerlessness, of appearing and remaining hidden.

At the beginning of July 1995 I am to spend a week at the convent, where a few guests at any one time may join the daily life of the community. I am looking forward to participating in the song and in the silence of the convent. I prepare by reading Lossky's *The Mystical Theology of the Eastern Church,* St Teresa's *Autobiography* and John Pick's biography of Gerard Manley Hopkins, *Gerard Manley Hopkins: Priest and Poet*, from 1942, which, in relating Hopkins' development to Loyola's *Exercises,* contrasts fundamentally with Norman White's recent biography, which concentrates on Hopkins' nature writing: both scholars read the life through the work and preserve the mystery of Hopkins' hiddenness while exploring his effectiveness and ineffectiveness as poet, as priest, as teacher, as friend, as family member.

The extent of the convent building and grounds is unexpected: the original buildings and more recent additions cover the span between two roads. They are flanked, on one side, by a large garden of grassy vista with benches for the nuns and, on the other, by a garden of winding paths and opulent rose bushes, which leads to the guest house, a small terraced house.

The room I am allocated looks out peacefully over this rose garden; and, below the small cross over a small shelf in a corner of the room, Sister Naomi has placed two roses of velvety vermilion complexity. The rose and the cross: 'There is the Rose: here dance!' Their fragrance fills the welcoming accommodation.

The daily regime sustains this first impression of sensuality, song and silence. From the visitors' chapel the plain chant of the nuns as they traverse Matins through Lauds, Terce, and Sext to None, Vespers and Compline, sounds in its round regularity like a choir of youthful angels, transforming even the most tumultuous psalms into the salve of the uncertain soul.

At dinner (lunch), the only meal of which guests partake with the nuns, the thirty-five nuns sit in a large rectangular refectory on immovable benches facing each other across the central section. The Mother Superior and her deputy sit at the top axis, and, at the other end of the three-sided tables, a nun reads from an edifying work of historical and political as well as spiritual interest. The light vegetarian meal is taken in silence: each nun has a spoon and fork but no knife. The food is prepared, served and cleared by the nuns themselves, who carry no more than two plates at a time, whether placing the dish on the table or clearing it away.

The nuns spend the mornings in domestic duties according to an allocated, circulating division of labour; after dinner there is a short rest period, and from None (2 p.m.) to High Tea (5.30 p.m.) and Vespers, they are relatively free to study, receive visitors, read, write letters. From Vespers (6 p.m.) to Compline (8.35 p.m.), a short, infinitely gentle service, there is also opportunity to converse. Then, marvellously, 'a *greater silence* is observed after Compline until after the Eucharist the next day'. Visitors are requested 'to please make silence and space for each other'. This swathe of greater silence spreads its sacrament with the setting sun over the sacred spaces of the convent – its passages and its impasses, its liturgical accesses and its witness to the damage and hope of the world beyond its confines.

One sister confides in me, eyes glinting with the pleasure of the secret shared, defused, 'I had an love affair with a Catholic priest, too.'

I am instantly at home here: the regimen of solitary concentration and meditation combined with communal activities does not feel very different from days spent in my study at home, or teaching and talking to colleagues at the university. The pace and rhythm of coming together and parting at regular intervals during day and night preserve the individuality and hiddenness of each nun, while offering her a framework of both formal support and friendships.

The exchange between Edna and myself is richer than ever: from Kant to St Augustine, to our fraught family histories, to the current state of British political parties, we are inexhaustible. I notice how, in the context of her convent, both Edna's irony – her distance from her community – and her irenicon – her peaceful immersion in its prayer and purpose – are accentuated.

In the wings of the morning, Psalm 139 searches me out: the hands of the living God are immersed in my reins, in my bowels, in my original knitting together: 'thou has covered me in my mother's womb'. This Hebrew news hold me and lets me go free, whereas the Greek aspiration to return the soul to its divine source fetters me for aeons in a body cursed and to be abandoned.

It is the grace of Edna that has given me this distinction between Hebrew and Greek, this insight into my condition – an insight which welds my medical and spiritual horizons, and which educates my confidence and my courage.

Edna tells me that the 'tranquil use' of *aporia*, in the classical Greek philosophy of Plato and in Aristotle, means literally 'no passage', hence philosophical difficulty or the lack of a resolution; it has a biblical equivalent of an altogether more drastic tone. In the Septuagint, the Greek translation of the Hebrew Scriptures, *aporia,* translates *behalah*, which means, 'dismay, sudden terror, or ruin'.

This biblical meaning of *aporia,* the sense of calamitous ruin – of destroying her relationship to her community and her hiddenness in prayer – was the ethical risk Edna put to me when I first revealed that I wanted to write about her.

May I dare to venture that she remains more truly hidden

because she gives of her ethical substance without stint, without counting the amount, because she is willing, whatever mistakes may be incurred, to make incursions into the damaged world for the sake of its denizens again and again. In this way the *aporia,* in both its Greek and its Hebrew versions, mutates towards the figure of the paradox, the knight of faith: a figure not assimilable either to a world-denying piety, nor to a world-immersed coercive power.

Only she who is truly hidden can truly enhance: only the powerless can wield power, power transcended by powerlessness.

Looking back, as I leave the convent in a taxi, through the entrance to the guest house, the convent has completely disappeared, the adjoining guest house has resumed its unremarkable place in the row of terraced houses. All I can see is the unbroken street of small undistinguished abodes. I am not the same person I was when I arrived. Where have I been? I settle back in the taxi with this companionable mystery of visibility and invisibility.

Margarets or Authority

RATIONAL THEOLOGY

The sowle is the precious Marguarite

(1450, KNT DE LA TOUR)

I have been expelled from Paradise, cruelly expelled, because it happened when I was visiting a Terrestrial Paradise, the gateway from the highest cornice of Purgatory to the heavenly realms.

Holidays can be terrible ordeals: instead of relaxing, relieved of the daily pressure of time and space and work and domestic labour, the restless soul may find itself even busier than ever. I have been travelling in Northern Italy with a – companion beset with the most remorseless *acedia* – laziness, sloth, apathy. Unable to acquiesce in her own being, her constant activity has its roots, paradoxically, in a deeper lack of will to action: that affirmation of the intensity of life which one finds – holding still – in whatever site surrounds one and whatever the soul sights in itself. A holiday drenched in sunshine and sea and air becomes the dark night of the soul, the foul womb of night, from which no birth into the uncreated light can issue.

And my witness to this pitiful despair, which I was powerless to assuage or even to address, was to fall into aridity myself. I had to expend so much of my energy protecting myself from the frantic insomnia of her days and nights, guarding myself from the accusations, voiced and unvoiced, of my distance where my ever-companionable daemon varies the beat of her dance, leading me and following me and casting rings about me, from which she may suddenly vanish, only to jump puckishly down or up again from the most unlikely abodes.

It was on my return that the true cost of the holiday bore down on me and burdened me. For only then, disengaged from proximity, could I fully acknowledge the scale of the disaster: hopelessness, lack of charity towards herself, fear of the faith that would lead along the path of despair to the walkways of ripening olive trees.

If you don't feel pain, you won't feel anything else.

My undesired anger at the damage such consistently disowned distress has caused me over the decades revived preoccupations which I want to believe I have overcome, so that, instead of having to protect myself from such emotional dishonesty, I can as far as possible simply affirm her and let her be, keeping her troubles quite distinct from my own needs and fears.

I fall into the Pelagian heresy – working strenuously to lift myself away from the voice of *ressentiment* that accompanied me night and day. This is, however, to try to exercise control over the emotion, and, in effect, it multiplies its points of access. But how to let go? Problems are never solved: they simply go away, they evaporate, and, one minute later, you wonder why you have found it so hard to emerge.

The releasing violence fell on me. My companion made it clear that she was not going to admit any difficulties on the holiday. How could she? For all emotional work – all the ironies and humour of failing each other – is inaccessible to her. So it was up to me to say unequivocally that I will not travel with her again. The tears were predictable, the coast not cleared, but the foreshore crossed. Some inkling of the real ventured. Ah, my dear, my dear, what *tristia saeculi*.

Autumn is here: there is no crispness in the air; the days deceive without a care, yet Autumn is here. Bosomy grapes throng the tray; the pears are turned in rich array. But where is my Friend? Oh where, oh where is my Friend?

I have come to you to greet you. My Margarets first met me with greetings: Margaret, when I arrived, trundled in a furniture van, in Brighton from Oxford, rushed down the stairs of the elegant regency bed-sitter mansion by the sea and introduced herself as also having arrived recently from Oxford to take up a teaching post at Roedean. Our affection burst out instantaneously. Margaret greeted me when I went for an interview for a Chair in Sociology at Warwick. She mentioned my colleague at Sussex, Tom Bottomore, and then told me boldly that I would count for two things in the department: to offer an alternative 'cultural' Marxism to the prevalent dogmatic Marxism; and also she wanted 'a Jew' to complement her Catholicism and the Anglicanism of the philosopher with whom she jointly taught an MA course. I found this unexpected brief thrilling and wrote to thank her for her greeting, regardless of whether I was appointed or not. When I joined the department I relished the resource of identity that could speak to the materialists and to the hidden ones and suffered no feelings of hypocrisy.

Margaret, Margarets. Why should I thread these two pearls of the soul together through my sinews? Not for any characteristics held 'in common': for their singularity, their uniqueness.

Vivo sin vivir en mi
Y de tal manera espero
Que muero porque no muero.

I live without living in myself
And in such a way I hope
I die because I do not die.

St Teresa's refrain of St John of the Cross,
Vivo Sin Vivir En Mí

The Margarets live in Paradise: equally, their *magis,* the 'more' of their illimitable love, is translated day by day into *caritas discreta,* the discretion of love. This 'discretion' is not a deluge of agapic love washing away the metaphysical tarns of Being and beings, as the post-modern theology of Jean-Luc Marion insists. *Caritas discreta* is intelligent: it discerns the negation that moves all love from the negation that keeps love from moving. *Caritas discreta* legitimates authority; it exercises a musical rationality which is itself always more − *magis.*

Margarets are tall, nay, lofty, with a posture of infinitely mobile and expressive shoulders: drawn back and down in receptivity, hunching forward with hilarity, set loose in pause and pensiveness.

Margarets are married: sacramental, spousal love, too, maybe even more, requires the exercise of the border between *magis* and *caritas discreta.* You could see the one marriage as the most morbid communion, the other as the most mutual communion. Yet Margarets live in Paradise. Paradise has to be entered as well as left again and again for it to be Paradise: the threshold of return runs through naked Hell and Purgatory; the threshold of egress is clothed with the apparel of the active intelligence.

Margarets refresh themselves frequently in the shifting pits of

40

the underworld. When they become impatient and patient with the perennial penance aroused by zealous ministrations towards others, which are invariably generous and effective, but which swell the soul to God-like dimensions, then prayer is the practice that arrests the pride: its repose softens the stiffened soul.

Margarets are human. Margaret wears full make-up, foundation, powder and rouge; Margaret has a scrubbed, luminous skin on which she lavishes the most expensive moisturisers. Margaret drinks vast quantities of middling red wine every evening; Margaret organises food and rest with her wonted devotion. Margarets have booming laughs – the paroxysm of pleasure drawn an octave lower in the throat than the speaking voice, not fading away but ceasing abruptly when the hilarity is spent.

Margarets occupy professional positions of great responsibility and conspicuousness: they are public people, sweeping majestically through the swarms of supplicants, employing support staff and training junior staff or students. They share the universal with all these classes of people in all its rigour and demand, while attending to the singularity of each individual, bestowing words or bestowing silence according to discernment.

Margarets know how to fail: to be tired, racy, snappy, hypercritical, impatient, usually on the way home, on arriving home, all evening. It is time to go down, to immerse one's soul and body in the brimming waters, however noxious and pestilential.

Here are three – my travelling companion, the Margarets – without narrative. There is no story to be told because these souls are perfected: the first mired in the swamp of *acedia,* Margarets with regularity in the refining furnaces of pain.

> *Que muero porque no muero.*
> I die because I do not die.

Dr Grove or Goodness

HELLENISM

What do you need to be a philosopher? You discover that you are a philosopher: it is not something you ever *become*.

Not a logical mind, not argumentative brio: philosophy is a passion. Discover this passion as a lover and witness of Socrates. Read the Platonic dialogues, *Phaedrus, Phaedo,* and the *Apology,* and you will fall in love with Socrates. You imbibe his frenzy, the madness of love inspired by Aphrodite and Eros. You feel you can reach out and touch the feathers that grow again from the roots all over the surface of the soul to ascend to divine beauty.

To be a philosopher you need only three things. First, infinite intellectual eros: endless curiosity about everything. Second, the ability to pay attention: to be rapt by what is in front of you without seizing it yourself, the care of concentration – in the way you might look closely, without touching, at the green lacewing fly, overwintering silently on the kitchen wall. Third, acceptance of pathlessness (*aporia*): that there may be no solutions to questions, only the clarification of their statement. Eros, attention, acceptance.

The much-touted 'end of philosophy', post-modernism, has sacrificed these connections by defining 'eros' as lack, 'attention' as deconstruction, 'acceptance' as mourning. This restricts instead of enlarging reason, which is maligned as sheer domination. Post-modernism amounts to a 'despairing rationalism without reason'.

42

In the name of new claimants, post-modernism protests on behalf of those who have been excluded from power, which is a highly rational endeavour: but, equally, it disqualifies any universal or shared notion of justice and the good. That is why I say that it is 'without reason' and 'in despair'. For how can you launch a claim without a communality? All versions of cultural pluralism suffer from this paradox.

Philosophy, as I understand and practice it, renews Socrates' search to explore the analogies between the soul, the city and the sacred. One of the ways this investigation has been carried out, from the pre-Socratic to the Hellenistic philosophers, has been by comparing the practice of philosophy with the practice of medicine: the philosopher tends the soul as the doctor tends the body. As the ancient world passed from the compass of city state to the metropolitan culture of imperial cities, the change in the political setting produced a change in the relation between authority and truth in both medicine and philosophy. If Hellenistic philosophy becomes more oriented to therapy, to aiding the individual soul in the relief of its delusion, medicine becomes more philosophical, aware of its limitations among the crowds and the clamour of the cosmopolitan climate.

I am not cured: I have had no remissions. My cancer is spreading around my body: it is in the lining of the bowel, it is in my lungs, it is in my pelvis. I do not have *health*: but I am *well*. How can that be?

A year ago, when I first developed effusions in the pleura (build-up of fluid in the lining of the lungs), which can be aspirated or tapped off, my local GP recommended that I see Dr Grove. He said, 'This is the person I would want to see if I had your condition.' In order to ensure that I did not lose the connection with Dr Land, who is at the forefront of international research into chemotherapy for ovarian cancer, I telephoned her to explain that, for the nonce, I intended to consult Dr Grove, who is based at a hospital in Coventry, not far from the university where I work.

Dr Land said slowly and measuredly, when I had explained the latest development in my condition: 'This means your cancer is active; this means you will become ill; this means you will need more treatment. How long do you intend to continue working?'

Disconcerted by her predictions, delivered in such apparently judicious tones, I went to see Dr Grove. He invited me to arrive after his clinic so that he could begin to get to know me. With a deliberate gesture, Dr Grove pushed aside the proliferating reports on my condition which littered his desk. I found myself looking into the smiley, impish eyes of a youthful forty-five-year-old with rounded shoulders, and, I would discover, a duck's waddle in his walk.

'Tell me,' he invited, 'who you are and how you are.'

I spoke for ten minutes and told him the whole story of how one consultant had told me the disease was progressing, while his colleague, with the same access to it, insisted that it was static.

Dr Grove examined me and then he said: 'You are well; you are not dominated by this disease; we will keep you in this equilibrium. Is there anything you want to do that you cannot do?'

The difference in the set of statements uttered by Dr Land and by Dr Grove is the difference between a sentence of death and a sentence of life.

Here philosophy provides the analogy for medicine. Dr Grove is able to say, 'I don't know:' 'I don't know what is causing this or that symptom.' 'I don't know what will happen next.' 'I don't know when you will die.' Dr Grove does not permit you to transfer your authority to him, and, so, paradoxically, you trust him more, because the trust is uncoerced and freely bestowed.

Dr Grove knows that you have to find your own way between what can be controlled and what can't be controlled; he never confuses that border with his own quest for control and fear of lack of control. Dr Grove has infinite eros: curiosity about each embodied soul he meets and treats; he pays the closest attention to everything they say to him. When I ask him if we can look at the X-rays of my lungs, he admonishes me gently but emphatically, 'Don't prejudice me by the prospect of the picture: I want to hear how you feel.' This is to incorporate the nursing definition of care into that of the specialist: not to ask first and foremost, 'What scientific map do we have of this body?' but to enquire, 'How do you feel? Can I make you feel more comfortable?' Finally, Dr Grove has acceptance: acceptance that there is no solution, no cure for this chronic illness, but also no finality: and that there is no need to find a surrogate prediction for this intrinsically limited knowledge.

Dr Grove invites you to carry your medical condition as *autopoeisis*: he said to me, 'Here are the various ways we can proceed. You decide which to adopt next, and *whatever you decide will be right*.' This way of presenting knowledge without arrogating authority but also without relinquishing it, means that each moment of the disease is alert to its equity, to the changing local and contingent considerations which affect its general course. *Autopoeisis*, the continuous inventing of the self, where that 'self' acquires infinite plasticity of boundary, is the gift of the doctor-philosopher who is skilled in bestowing the truth or reason and the authority of his discipline onto his patient, or, rather onto his synergist, his co-agent. If the Stoics sought to relieve people of their deluded beliefs which occlude the soul, this doctor-philosopher effects a more complete mediation, for his strategy transfers the knitting of body and soul back to me.

I have lost most of my hair. Losing my long, heavy tresses of hair has been the motif of one of two recurrent nightmares as long as I can remember. In the dream I have had my hair cut, or I have left my home for cramped accommodation. The dream always begins at the same point, the *fait accompli*: I never go through the process of decision and operation. It is done. The panic sets in at the sudden realisation of what has been done. I don't know what the symbolism is of losing the hair: the symbolism of losing the home is simple. It reverts to the loss of two homes on the occasion of the two divorces; and my guilt, conscious in the second case, of having so ardently desired to leave home and strike out on my own. As for the hair? Could it be the symbol of feminine power – hair to catch and petrify men? Or is it the longing for security – hair to hide in? Am I sworn to the Gorgon or to Artemis?

Over the six months from January to June 1995, my hair comes out in lumps when I wash it, and it sheds itself profusely all day long. Wispy and spasmodic, my remaining hair no longer affords the camouflage for my faces or the arsenal for my graces. Dr Grove eliminates the drug which causes hair loss from the cocktail of chemotherapy I am currently undergoing: it makes no difference, the hair continues to fall out.

One Monday night I watch on television a programme about teenagers who have cancer. Usually avoiding such programmes – I refuse to identify with cancer as a generality – this programme draws me. How can such young people, about to begin in so many ways, respond to this condition?

With wisdom, it seems, Forming an association, these largely bald young people have each as individuals acquired a daunting maturity, compounded of determination and humility. How eyes shine and smiles expand without the frame of hair – the contours of the visage reveal the sap of the engaged and willing soul.

The unaccustomed clarity of countenance entreasures their brave poverty of spirit.

I no longer mind about losing my hair and become curious about my new appearance – about time I had the courage to wear less hair. Maybe I'll find a better way, too, to remain hidden.

Jonathan or Sephardism

HOLOCAUST ANTHROPOLOGY

> *Was I born to become*
> *A ritual mourner?*
> *I want to sing of festivities,*
> *The greenwood into which Shakespeare*
> *Often took me.*

CZESLAW MILOSZ, In Warsaw, 1945

The Palace at Łancut, pronounced 'Wantzut', in eastern Galicia, set in formal grounds, punctuated with marble obelisks spread-eagle finialed, and with swagged urns on elaborately carved pedestals, presents an immaculate facade. The horizontal rhythm of the huge first-floor fenestration is arrested by pavilions at either end, their grey long-and-short-work cornerstones against white stucco climbing one third up. They are crowned with blue metallic onion cupolas and an ultimate shooting star on a thin rod. A row of rams' heads engage the architrave of the pastel orangery in a riot of Adamesque familiar regularity.

Inside we have rented three rooms for the night. They are inexpensive, and there is a toilet down the corridor. It is by far the best sanitation we shall enjoy on this week in Galicia, but it is not pleasant. Jonathan had booked a bus for the dozen or so participants at 'The Future of Auschwitz' Conference who had expressed eagerness to spend a week travelling from Kraków to

Belzec, through south-east Galicia, to visit the second death camp, but, more importantly, to trace with him the route of holocaust ethnography that he has single-handedly invented and launched. With great good humour, Jonathan used me to inform the Americans that we could stay in Soviet hotels or we could stay in Polish castles and 'palaces'. The hotels would be soulless slabs with private facilities; the Polish residences would have history and character, with indifferent shared facilities. He predicted that no one would come; I was disbelieving and clambered around the bus that took us to and from Kraków to Auschwitz with the tidings. One by one the others dropped out. Extraordinary things occurred: telegrams arrived from the States with news of a spouse's sudden illness, phone messages were left pressing urgent academic exigencies. Jonathan cancelled the bus and hired a car for himself, Priscilla his conference organiser and personal assistant, and myself. He said he would keep his commitment even if only one person remained.

In the evening in the palace at ancut, after a meagre meal, the three of us sat on the narrow beds in one of the shabby, sparsely-furnished large rooms with a great slab of milk chocolate and a bottle of Polish vodka, which is much drier than Russian vodka. It was early April 1992, the air was raw and my skin felt abraided, doubtless part of my complex response to the almost unendurable curiosity and pain of being in Poland, only made bearable by the warm and intelligent fellowship of Priscilla and Jonathan.

Soviet slab monuments, slabs of hotels, slabs of chocolate. Jonathan has the most haunting, heart-rending voice. Standing in the front tower-room overlooking the whole site of Birkenau, he raised his voice and he deepened it as he led the lamentation. In the non-operatic manner of the *Baal Tefilah* by contrast with the more operatic style of the *Hazan,* this cantor intones the sacred Hebrew consonants as they were first written, without inserting vowels and without punctuation, so that each mystic word has its own unique chant. 'Uniqueness' is the thing that Jonathan's universal intelligence is able to resonate in so many ways. The sound came from a place, from a time, where the celestial height and the abyssal depths violate their conflux.

January 1994, Jonathan and Connie are to be married. The wedding ceremony will take place at the unique Bevis Marks Synagogue, the oldest Spanish and Portuguese synagogue in London, off Leadenhall Street in the East End. Built in 1701, 'Bevis Marks' was known as 'Gate to Heaven', and indeed Connie and Jonathan took us through the gate to heaven on their wedding day, which was a holy day and a holiday. Yet Jonathan also took me on another holy day: through the gates surmounted by the Bauhaus lettering *Arbeit Macht Frei* at Auschwitz *Stammlager* One. Auschwitz is not 'the ineffable' to him: it is inscription, codification, myth, organisation; it is comprehension.

'Auschwitz' is not simply Jewish death: Auschwitz happened in the midst of the great vibrant culture of Jewish art. Yes, *art*: the people who ban images, who forbid representation of God, are a people of artists: they sing, they sing in turquoise synagogues thronged with natural representations, while the cemeteries with their funerary monuments and representations are the basic institution of the community, humorously de-scribed, with a more than euphemistic nuance, as 'the place of meaning for all who are alive'. This is the middle, broken indeed, between the two gates to Heaven and to Hell, the mount of purgation.

I am phobic about weddings: I long for my wedding, and weddings make me feel murderous and wretched. Jonathan and Connie arrange 'A Wedding Coach' to depart from St Giles, Oxford, outside the Taylorian, on that January Sunday at 1.30 p.m., to take guests to the Bevis Marks Synagogue and from there to the Glaziers' Hall for the reception. It will leave London for Oxford at 11 p.m.. The 'wedding coach' is already the orange-saturated pumpkin, magicked into an iridescent glass globe in which miracles will occur – but only if one observes strictly the hours specified for its voyage out into eternity and back. The art of this wedding is unsurpassable. The invitation in the shape of a tabernacle with a central opening is adorned on the outside with a gold and white engraving heralded with pairs of mythical beasts. At the bottom of the central candelabrum, out of which sprout the riverline leaves and shady umbels of a tree, two winged gryphons protrude merry tongues beyond their beaky heads, while two smaller contrapposto lions, also splayed across the central seam, turn their heads to grasp wayward tendrils in their maws against their flowing manes. Inside the ark there is an *epithalamion* in Hebrew. 'Epithalamion' is a Greek word for the genre of wedding poem: it means literally 'before the bed'. The Hebrew equivalent could be called *shirey kallah/hatan* – 'bridge/groom' poems, or *shirey keluloth* – 'espousal' poems. This poem was composed by Raphael Loewe in medieval Sephardi Hebrew style, subject to the classical discipline regarding prosody and vocabulary – rare and extraordinary benison.

בס״ד

ראו רעים, בשורת יום חתנה   וְשִׂמְחַת לב, וקול חתן וכלה,

פצו פיכם בשיר מזמור והודו   בקול רנה לא׳ל נורא עלילה,

א׳להים הוא אשר מושיב יחידים,   יהונתן, וחיה הבתולה

שמו מאיר, ושם אביו יהודה,   שמה שרה, לאמנו משולה,

הלא היא בת ישעיהו, עליהם   לחפה תהיה כבוד דגולה

ביום אחד בשבת יקחה לו   לסדר "והייתם לי סגלה",

בא״י-זה יום לחדש הדלי, בו   שעת ארבע, עלות מנחה תפלה,

בבית מקדש מעט, גולי ספרד   יסדוהו לחדש שם קהלה

שמו שער לשמים, מקומו   בבייריש מארקס לעיר לונדריש כלילה.

ומשסדרו שבע ברכות   ילוום כל-קריאיהם בגילה,

לעבר מנהר טמש לסעודה,   לשם מצוה, שתיה גם אכילה,

באולם חושבי ציור זכוכית: לכו, שמחו, וצפו לגאלה,

והודו לאשר שמח יצירו   בעדן – לו לבדו הגדלה,

ותפארת, והנצח, וההוד,   מרומם על ברכה אף תהלה

The above Hebrew poem was specially composed as the invitation to the wedding of Connie Wilsack and Jonathan Webber. It was written in Hebrew by Raphael Loewe, emeritus professor of Hebrew at University College, London. The translation on the opposite page and the explanatory notes on pages 54–5 were prepared by Connie and Jonathan Webber at Gillian Rose's request some months later.

By the grace of God

See here, friends, the announcement of a wedding,
Heartfelt rejoicing, the voice of bride and groom.
Open your mouths wide in triumphal paean
And give thanks in joyful voice to the God of wondrous deeds –
God who settles singles into pairs –
In this case Jonathan and Chaya.
He the son of Judah is, his name renowned as the giver of light,
She known also as Sarah, the daughter of Isaiah, and to
                                        our matriarch alike –
Great glory will attend their wedding ceremony
On Sunday, day one of 'You shall be to me a treasure' week,
The eleventh or so day in the Aquarian month
At the afternoon prayer at four o'clock
In the miniature sanctuary of Bevis Marks
Where exiles from Spain renewed their community in
                                        London's city walls –
'Gate to Heaven', they called it.
And when the seven ritual blessings have been duly said
Let their guests accompany them with joy
Across the River Thames for the ritual feast –
Drinking and dining in the glass-etchers' hall.
Go, rejoice, and await the Redemption,
And thank the One who brought joy to his creation in Eden –
To Him alone, exalted above all blessing and beyond all praise,
Is the greatness, the splendour, the glory, and the majesty.

Notes to the Translation

friends   The Hebrew echoes the text of the sixth of the seven ritual blessings at the wedding ceremony.

heartfelt rejoicing   The numerical value of the Hebrew letters is equivalent to the year according to the Jewish calendar (5754).

voice of bride and groom   The Hebrew echoes the text of the last of the seven ritual blessings at the wedding ceremony.

in joyful voice   Literally, in the voice of joy (Ps. 118:15).

the God of wondrous deeds   The opening phrase and refrain of a well-loved liturgical poem sung in the Spanish and Portuguese tradition at the *ne'ilah* service on Yom Kippur.

Chaya   The first of Connie's two Hebrew names.

the son of Judah   Jonathan's father's Hebrew name.

his name renowned as the giver of light   The second of Jonathan's two Hebrew names is 'Meir', literally, 'gives light'.

Sarah   The second of Connie's two Hebrew names.

the daughter of Isaiah   Connie's father's Hebrew name.

'You shall be to me a treasure' week   The weekly Torah reading on the Sabbath following the wedding contains the phrase 'You shall be to me a treasure' (Exod. 19:5), referring to God's promise to the Children of Israel at the giving of the Torah on Mount Sinai.

The eleventh or so day in the Aquarian month   Literally, 'some day in the Aquarian month', but this is a play on words, as the Hebrew for 'some' contains the letters *alef* and *yod* that signify eleven, the date of the wedding in the Jewish month of Shevat, corresponding to Aquarius in the zodiac.

in the miniature sanctuary   A synagogue is perceived as a miniature sanctuary, representing the Holy Temple.

Bevis Marks   The name of the street in the City of London where the synagogue is located.

Where exiles from Spain renewed their community   Jews were allowed back to Britain only in the middle of the seventeenth century. The synagogue in Bevis Marks was established by refugees from Spain and Portugal in 1701. The term used for London, 'Londresh', reflects the Portuguese pronunciation.

'Gate to Heaven'   A literal translation of the name of the synagogue.

glass-etchers' hall   A reference to the Glaziers' Hall, a guild hall in the City of London.

the seven ritual blessings   Of the wedding ceremony.

with joy   The Hebrew again echoes the last of the seven ritual blessings at the wedding ceremony.

Across the River Thames   The synagogue is to the north of the Thames, the Glaziers' Hall to the south. The term used for the Thames, 'Temsh', again reflects the Portuguese pronunciation.

for the ritual feast   In fulfilment of a rabbinical injunction.

the One who brought joy to his creation in Eden   The Hebrew echoes the text of the sixth of the seven ritual blessings at the wedding ceremony.

the greatness, the splendour, the glory, and the majesty (1 Chron. 29:11).

The juxtaposition in this poem of numerologies and calendars – biblical, talmudic, liturgical, zoharic, zodiac – echoes their juxtaposition on the frescoed walls of the ruined and restored synagogues of Galicia.

The journey down to London was the journey back to Whitechapel; back to my grandparents' narrow dark wholesaler's shop where, in their teens, they had sold the imperfect stockings discarded by the sweat-shops in the vicinity, until they accumulated enough capital to start acting as 'middlemen' between the stocking factories and the retailers. The contrast between the skyscrapers and the hutches seems only to guarantee the immortality of the route in a cinematic vision through the high, protective window of the coach.

We arrive at the Bevis Marks Synagogue at half-past three. It is already dusk. The wedding ceremony is to be part of the regular afternoon service. The exterior of the building has the simple proportions of dissenters' chapels of the period, 1701, when it was completed. Inside it is sumptuous: with high rounded windows reflecting the light provided solely by candles in the seven brass chandeliers and the *Ner Tamid,* the eternal lamp. The width of the window recesses reveal the thickness of the walls, and the carved furnishings on which we sit longitudinally facing the men are made of the darkest, thickest wood. The *bimah,* the platform on which the reader's desk is placed for the reading of the Torah, is in front of the Ark, flanked by rows of separated men and women. The wooden Ark resembling a reredos, the ornamental screen covering the wall at the back of an altar, is classically baroque, with the Ten Commandments in Hebrew. We have indeed entered a timeless, burnished, chiaroscuro Baroque, which seems apt for the Sephardic congregation. Our finery, furs and hats and jewels, has changed like the pumpkin into the costume of southern European Jewry of that bygone era.

At quarter to four the choral service begins, the choir invisible at an upper level, plangent in their call to prayer. The service in Hebrew begins at four o'clock, the only part spoken in English concerning the business of the wedding contract, uninhibitedly assimilated into the holy service. Jonathan reads the Torah with the two presiding Rabbis. Four forty-five and still no bride. Then the far door to our right opens, and a bridesmaid appears leading the procession which includes the bride, other bridesmaids, the bride's immediate family. The chief bridesmaid carries a *menorah,* the candelabrum with seven branches, high in front of her face. The candles waft on the air of their own accord, their shadowy bearer, her face almost invisible, a billowing angel misted in floating garments. The aureoles of the different darkness deepen, the plumes of dancing light fall on the long-awaited bride. Connie always has the most dignified bearing; she carries herself with confidence and grace. Lightly veiled and dressed in a suit with a nacreous sheen, a neat jewelled cap on her head, she enters the *bimah*. The service continues in Hebrew, with little resonance of merry Ashkenazi weddings under the *Huppah*, the bridal canopy, when the bridegroom joyously breaks the glass under his heel. This wedding has an altogether different pathos. Joy, yes, but solemn, with the recognition, suffered in the Baroque shadows, of sufferance, survival, of the tides of time which still await the Redemption.

> To him alone, exalted above all blessing and
> beyond all praise,
> Is the greatness, the splendour, the glory and
> the majesty.

'The place of meaning for all who are alive.' Funerary furniture is a fundamental form of Jewish art and expression. The ethnography of Galicia is inscribed in these remnants, whose condition varies in the same way as the synagogues: from the synagogue at Rymanów where the crumbling, roofless walls alternate bare brick with eroded pointing and Hebrew lettering frescoed in blind alcoves, the sacred letters booming out and shrinking into unfathomable silence, to the glories of Łancut. There, in the restored synagogue, the walls, shimmering in turquoise, with architraves banded in blues and reds and brilliant ochre, surround arcaded medallions of zodiac creatures, the lion, the leopard, the deer, scorpions and the eagle, and frescoed vistas of countryside and towers, interspersed with the painted arks of Hebrew. The central *Bimah* is flanked by four massive round gold-speckled piers, harbouring at their apex the messianic Leviathan eating its tail and skin in preparation for the Messianic Age.

Jonathan shows us the fate of gravestones throughout Galicia: he has found them used in retaining walls, for paving streets, in children's playgrounds, in the proximity of concrete, residential tower blocks, forming paths up hillsides. These discoveries are not the silent witness of the foreign ethnographer: every gravestone that Jonathan meets talks to him. Invariably even revisiting gravestones he had already identified on previous visits conjured up a new informant. People tend the stones, or someone would emerge as we debouched on them heeding some call that Jonathan had issued without any audible appeal. With his excellent Polish he would engage his interlocutor and a history would unravel – some account of survival, of return, of *inheritance,* afforded by the existence, however disguised or hidden, of these articulate stones.

The Nazis always ordered the destruction of the cemeteries, understanding that they represented the future, the continuity of the generations, as much as children and grandchildren. However, at Tarnów the massive cemetery is intact, with new, wrought-iron gates and a fence and wall. We also found gravestones forming part of the retaining wall at the main Post Office in the centre of the town, as if they had migrated back to the Rynek, the market square where the Jews were shot over two days and buried under the street, which was said to heave with movement for months after. At Debica we walked through the barren housing estates to find tombstones in whirlpools of acute angles in a corner of a playground, blithely ignored by the scrambling children. They had been hurled together in the hope that the earth would suck them back into her element. At Przeworsk the Jewish cemetery is now the main bus station, while at Lubaczów the cemetery is magnificently intact on the hillside periphery of the town. At Kánczuga we follow a path of tombstones around a farm to the former hillside cemetery. At Lesko the cemetery dates from the seventeenth century, but we find stones from the sixteenth century, too.

The stones, in addition to their inscriptions, are highly decorated. Many are surmounted by the three crowns, the crown of kingship, the crown of priesthood and the crown of a good name, against a background of scumbled polychromy. Others have blessing hands which indicate priests' tombstones, while a jug and bowl signify tombstones of the Levites, who washed the priests' hands before blessing. The image of a hand throwing coins into an alms-box means that the dead helped the poor. To my delight I saw numerous bookcases, because a very pious Jew devotes his spare time to study. Women's tombstones are usually decorated with candelabra, because it is their duty to light the candles. Jonathan deciphers an inscription: 'Let her soul join the circle of eternal life.'

These necropolises give us the Jewish polity and Jewish proximity: the universal political community and the bare bones of each particular existence. They mediate between the generations by preserving and transcending the public politics of daily negotiation and the household gods of daily communion, between business and repose, between the prose of neighbourliness and the poetry of intimacy. Their continuity forms a counterbalance to those forlorn suitcases, chalked with the surname, town and date of birth in the gigantic glass tanks at the Museum in Auschwitz-One which furnish the funerary monuments for those who were slaughtered in the camp.

Once the marriage of Connie and Jonathan is solemnised, the wondrous deeds of the ritual feast commence. The coach deposited us across London Bridge at the Glaziers' Hall in Montague Close in the precincts of Southwark Cathedral. Two hundred guests deposited their coats and ascended the stairway to the glass-etchers' hall. From the ceiling of the huge hall, set with myriad round tables, hangs a host of heavenly chandeliers. Splaying down, the candles are bedizened with festoons and bubbles, and the light is as opulent as the feast – no soft suggestion to seed the potential romances among the guests. The members of the wedding have been translated from the shimmering libration of the bride's guiding candelabrum, the fractional lights of the messianic promise, to these chandeliers, cataracts of overhead light, the wide, daring blaze of hope fulfilled.

The menu has been composed with ethnographic precision: we are to begin with Brzostek Winter Fantasy, an array of winter leaves garnished with wild mushrooms, asparagus tips and rye *croûtons*, with hazelnut vinaigrette. Wild mushrooms and rye grow in abundance in Poland. This is followed by Great Clarendon Consommé, a 'double' consommé garnished with a julienne of vegetables, accompanied by nori twists, Japanese puff-pastry and seaweed. Then the entrée is Viandes Copacabana, poussins stuffed with rice, pine kernels, raisins and apricots, accompanied by Purim peppers and courgette fleur. This dish alludes to the discovery that complex Sephardi dishes originating in Haleb (Aleppo) in Syria are a key feature of Jewish festive meals in the Copacabana district of Rio de Janeiro, Brazil. The courgette fleur and spinach-stuffed Purim peppers are so called because the dish is always a riot of colour, reminiscent of the carnival celebrations at Purim. Finally, Sunset Sof Ma'arav, fresh strawberries accompanied by caramel oranges set on a raspberry coulis, accompanied by crêpes suzette. The tinkling of the wine goblets seems orchestrated by the maestros of glass and light soaring above us. The contralto music of two hundred revellers' voices circulates with increasing volume around the tables. The wedding of two mature people has the quality of supreme success unbiddable by young couples.

My magic holiday continued. I was seated between Jonathan Israel and Nicholas de Lange, both of whose work I knew but whom I had never met. Present as guests of the bride Connie, who is the editor of the distinguished Littman Library of Jewish Civilization, to which they act as consultants, they both provided excellent conversation as the charmed coach drew further and further out into the glorious empyrean.

Jonathan has invited a team of roving gypsy players, the Lawutara Group, from Tarnów, and they provide jolly background strings as well as an interlude of song and dance. After the many toasts, the bride leads traditional Jewish dancing, which never fails to be plangent in all its boisterousness – Jewish joy soaked and soaring with the wings of accumulated suffering. My two companions crown the occasion and open vistas to me in spite of the unvarying, dazzling light of this Paradise, which obliterates the passing of time – even though we know that our clothes will turn to rags at the stroke of eleven.

Jonathan and Connie have translated the arts of Polish and worldwide Jewry into the vehicle of their wedding, just as Jonathan finds the art of life at the centre of his holocaust anthropology.

On the long coach journey back to Oxford I sink anonymously into the dark night, and revel, all the way, in the sentiment of having been transported by the difference of a day – of having relished every aspect of a wedding.

The tree is really rooted in the sky.

SIMONE WEIL, *Gravity and Grace*

To be a Sephardi Jew and to be an anthropologist is to combine orthodoxy and exile. It is in the orthodox synagogues that the rules are relaxed: people pray and they gossip, children of both sexes roam around, are given sweets; if a women's head is uncovered, it means that she is unmarried. In the Reform Synagogue the rule is strict, because it is less customary and there is no definite assurance that it will be universally known. Learned improvisation is the hallmark of both orthodoxy and anthropology.

The tree is really rooted in the sky.

This is not a mystical appeal to the ineffability of the sky, but a relating of gravity and grace:
It is the light falling continuously from

heaven which alone gives a tree the energy to
send powerful roots deep into the soil.

The pathos of gravity – of weight, ground, earth, city –
channelled to grace – the response to ethical commandment –
means that spiritual and religious life, supernatural, is not
radically divorced from nature, being, logic and politics.

The tree is really rooted in the sky.

What courage is summoned by this icon of the visible and the
invisible. To be a tree. To be suspended in the empyrean, with
no security, no identity, no community. Yet only this willing-
ness to be suspended in the sky, to be without support, enables us
to draw on the divine source and sustenance which makes it
possible to put down roots. It is not the prior fixity of established
roots that qualify us to drink greedily out of the sky. The sky is
universal – it is the silky canopy that moves with us wherever we
go. And we feel lost, we are in the abyss; and the sky has become
dark and occluded, we need to pull up those roots for the
channel of grace is run dry. We need to venture again the
courage of suspense, not knowing who we are, in order to
rediscover our infinite capacity for self-creation and response to
our fellow self-creators. Orthodoxy embraces exile. The three
lights of the future, the eternal present, the past: the promise of
the candelabrum, the blazing fulfilment of the chandeliers, the
sky guarding over gravestones and drawing trees. Three gates to
heaven bestow their virtue onto the earth.